.

THE COUPLE'S ACTIVITY BOOK

70 INTERACTIVE GAMES
TO STRENGTHEN YOUR RELATIONSHIP

THE COUPLE'S ACTIVITY BOOK

CRYSTAL SCHWANKE

ROCKRIDGE
PRESS

To Ryan: Thanks for encouraging me and
joining me in the silliness for all these years.
Love you.

Interior and Cover Designer: Angie Chiu
Art Producer: Hannah Dickerson
Editor: Anne Lowrey
Production Editor: Matt Burnett

Illustrations © Bett Norris 2020, cover and pp. ii, ix, x, 10, 15, 20, 22, 30, 35, 38, 45, 47, 48, 52, 57,
58, 63, 66, 74, 84, 94, 102, 109, 113, 114, 117, 123, 124, 132; Creative Market/Ekaterina Kiriy, p. 79;
Icons used throughout courtesy of the Noun Project: supplies (pencil) by Maxim Basinski, stopwatch
by Atif Arshad, thumbs up by Gregor Cresnar, camera by James Kopina, dice by Christopher T.
Howlett.

ISBN: Print 978-1-64611-991-2 | eBook 978-1-64611-992-9
R0

Contents

Introduction

Hi there! I'm Crystal Schwanke, freelance writer and former editor of LoveToKnow.com's dating channel. I studied psychology because I have always had a passion for helping people reach their potential. I chose to apply it with the written word to inspire people and help them connect—including in romantic relationships. For 16 years, I've been married to a man who encourages me to be silly and participates in any of the games, song parodies, or other activities I come up with, without even flinching. We've given each other the freedom to be ourselves without fear of judgment, no matter how goofy we want to be. We celebrate the zaniness and it helps keep us close (and keeps me out of my shell, which is no small feat since I'm naturally pretty shy).

So many of us operate on autopilot, even in our most important relationships. It's easy to overlook games and activities as things that can help your relationship thrive. You know that saying, "All work and no play makes Jack a dull boy"? It's true for relationships, too. If you're just going to work, running errands, discussing chores, and then zoning out in front of the television for "fun," you're missing a whole level of connection that can bring a sense of levity back to your relationship. Even if you go out on official date nights that give you a break from day-to-day demands, you could find yourself stuck in a rut, too. Dinner, check. Movie, check. Show a little affection because you know it falls through the cracks during the weeks, check.

It's time to interact with each other in a way that may be brand-new to the two of you! Within these pages, you'll find a mix of activities that you can do together while face-to-face. Some you can do at home, while others allow or encourage you to venture out together. You'll also find that many of these can be done over the phone/video chat. Whether someone is temporarily out of town or you're in a long-distance relationship (for now), you'll have a variety of fun new ways to connect.

In some cases, you're even prompted to spread that lighthearted joy of being in love. Go into these activities seeking *true* connection without a serious ulterior motive. This isn't a cure-all for healing a relationship or an activity to mend your bond right after you've had a fight. This is all about genuinely enjoying each other's company while celebrating your love for each other. The aim of this book is pure, carefree fun while you get to know each other on a new level.

Because relationships can change so much over time, it can be easy to sometimes feel you've become more like roommates or, at times, even strangers. This is perfectly normal, but it's a good reason to regularly reconnect with your significant other and actively nurture the fun elements of your lives—even if it's just for five minutes after dinner or once the kids are in bed. Using activities like these to joke, get creative, explore each other's minds, and just have fun together can help you feel connected. Strengthening your relationship gets to be fun, exciting, and lighthearted! I hope that each time you use this book, you'll both walk away feeling lighter, happier, and more connected as a couple.

How to Use This Book

I designed this book in a way that'll allow you to choose your own adventure as a couple. You can flip to a particular theme based on your mood or open it randomly and let chance decide your activity. You can also work through the whole thing from cover to cover. There are no rules.

If you see a game you like but you want to tweak it to make it more personal to you and your significant other, please do. This whole book is about you and enjoying your relationship, so feel free to do whatever helps you make the most of it!

You should be able to do any of these games and activities when you're spending time together in person. If you're in a long-distance relationship or can only call or video chat one evening, there are still things you can do together to get out of a rut—"How was your day?" "Good. Yours?" "Same." Pose some questions (other than *that* one), play a silly game of fill-in-the-blank, or just do random word associations until it just gets too ridiculous or funny to keep going.

While a lot of these activities are perfect for a night at home (even on weeknights!), you can also use some of the games during road trips or on other outings around town. Some of the games will require you to go out in public but only for as long as you want. You can even weave

some of them into your day-to-day activities if errands and household chores make up a large chunk of the time you get to spend together. (Hey, some couples have less time than others, especially with small children or two hectic jobs—I totally get it.) It's important to connect with your significant other as often as possible, so there are some activities here that are conversation only, allowing you to do them anywhere, and some that shouldn't take more than 10 minutes.

I recommend keeping a pencil or pen and some scrap paper nearby as you engage with this book. Although it is not required, you may even want to have a blank journal to record all of your antics!

My hope is that you can return to this book nightly, weekly, or on special occasions when you have unexpected time together and don't know what to do with it. Maybe you receive a fortuitous babysitting offer or your work schedules happen to align perfectly for an evening. Whether you have been together for two months or twenty years, use this book to bring fun, lightness, laughter, and even discovery to your relationship.

I made this book just for you two. Now it's your turn to make it your own!

MARKER
make a cocktail!
BINGO!
FREE!
NEWS!
watch T.V.!
take out the trash!

CHAPTER ONE

Silly

Spontaneous moments of silliness are great whenever you are feeling playful or even just when you want to lighten the mood. Silly activities also often give you plenty of inside jokes to enjoy together even after a game or activity is over.

This chapter has everything from wordplay to a game of bingo (that may end with a kiss) to a throwback to Simon Says. If you're in the mood to be a little goofy with your significant other without much of a time commitment, start here.

A Fill-in-the-Blanks Story

SUPPLIES NEEDED:
Pen or pencil

ESTIMATED TIME:
5 minutes

This activity will hopefully inspire some laughs as you work together to create a zany micro story. Who knows what direction you'll take this in together! You can repeat it as often as you like—the story will be different every time.

INSTRUCTIONS

1. Decide which one of you will be the one to see the story ahead of time. Don't let your partner see the story before all the blanks are filled!

2. That person will call out each word prompt listed under each blank line, in order. Allow your partner to speak what comes to mind and write it down in the corresponding blank space.

3. Read the letter out loud at the end, once all the blanks are filled.

Dear _____,
Name of partner with the book right now

I am SO _____ we met at _____ when we did that _____
        emotion   place   activity

in the _____. My life has been full of _____ and _____
     season   emotion   emotion

since then. And to think, when I woke up that morning, I was in such

a _____ mood. It was so nice to find someone to talk about
   emotion

_____ with! I felt like you totally _____ me. Here's
     topic   verb, past tense

something I've never told you: The _____ I wore that day is now
                                      article of clothing

my lucky _____. Now I always wear it when I _____.
      article of clothing   verb

I can't wait for the day when we _____ together. My favorite memory
                                  verb

so far is when we _____ at _____. You were so
                  verb, past tense   place

_____!
  adjective

Did you think I was _____? I sure hope so.
                  adjective

Sincerely,

_____
Name of partner without the book right now

P.S. On our next date, we should go out for _____ and watch
                                       food

_____. I'll wear my _____ _____ and
      movie   color   article of clothing

maybe you can wear your _____ _____.
                    color   article of clothing

What're You Going to Do?

SUPPLIES NEEDED:

Paper or card stock

Scissors

Pen or pencil

Jar or bowl

Several small objects (coins, pebbles, or scraps of paper)

ESTIMATED TIME: 30 to 45 minutes, including time to make the cards and boards

This is a game of bingo for two with a twist.

INSTRUCTIONS

1. You need two different bingo boards and a set of "bingo balls" to play. Using the paper or card stock, make two copies of the bingo board on the next page: Cut one into squares, then fold them with the writing inside to serve as "bingo balls." Use the other as a board.

2. Make an additional board by changing the order of the squares or adding new squares. If a task appears on a board, it will also need a "bingo ball."

3. Put the "bingo balls" in a jar or bowl and take turns pulling tasks from the jar, reading them aloud, and performing the action. Whoever has a match on their board can put a small object on that space on the board (use a pencil to mark it off if you don't have enough pennies, pebbles, etc.).

4. The first person to get a straight line in any direction wins and immediately stands to perform their goofiest victory dance. The other partner has to perform the last task that was called.

Use this template to create a bingo board.

Kiss my cheek	You do the dishes	1-Minute back massage	Make me a drink	Let me plan the next date
Sing something	Make me laugh	Staring contest	Kiss forehead	Take out the trash
You plan the next date	Name 1 reason you like me	**FREE**	1-Minute foot massage	Compliment me
Recite a poem	Kiss lips	Name something that scares you	Write me a note and hide it for later	Make a silly face
Name something that makes you happy	Talk to me in a funny voice/ accent	Rub your belly and pat your head	Take a photo with me	Let me choose what we watch next

Word Associations

 **SUPPLIES NEEDED:**
Timer (from an old board
game or your phone)

 ESTIMATED TIME: As long
as you'd like to spend on it

This is a fun and fast-paced game that can be done anywhere. Include
a few rounds of this game during a walk, on a car ride, over the phone,
while doing chores around the house, or while spending time together
on the couch.

INSTRUCTIONS

1. Set a timer for 1 minute.

2. One person says a random word. Then, the other partner has to say
   the first word that comes to mind—no filters. The first player then
   says the first word that pops into their head.

3. Keep going back and forth until time is up. You never know where
   you'll end up, but you might find yourselves sharing stories between
   words for a chuckle. ("What? How did you get to *that* word from
   that one?") You can also continue this without a timer if you want to
   keep playing!

Here's a quick example:

Partner 1: Coffee

Partner 2: Cup

Partner 1: Cupcake

Partner 2: Birthday

TIP: Add a rule to make things more challenging. For example, all words
could have to fit into a specific category, start with the same letter,
rhyme, etc.

Sweetheart Says

🖊 **SUPPLIES NEEDED:**
Pen
Paper

⏱ **ESTIMATED TIME:**
10 minutes

Use your personal and/or private nicknames to play this take on Simon Says. The game tests your listening skills and prompts you to pay close attention to each other's words. The skills you practice here will serve you well during both casual and more serious conversations. For now, it's all in good fun! Depending on your mood and creativity, this one has the potential to be as hilarious and/or romantic as you'd like.

INSTRUCTIONS

1. Choose who will go first. If you have nicknames you've given each other, use them.

2. Have one partner instruct the other to do whatever they want, no matter how silly. It's the moment you've been waiting for, right? **The only rule is that they can only follow instructions if it starts with their nickname.**

Say things like:

> [Nickname] says, "Kiss my cheek."

> [Nickname] says, "Go grab a couple of drinks from the fridge and choose a movie for later."

> [Nickname] says, "Tell me what your perfect weekend looks like."

> "Give me the weirdest, on-command laugh you can muster. Do it until I can't help but laugh, too."

3. Notice that the last command didn't begin with a nickname. If someone completes an instruction without a nickname, they lose.

4. Each correctly completed instruction gets a point. Using the pen and paper, keep score of how many rounds they get through before they lose, then switch roles and see who can go the longest before making a mistake.

Read My Face

SUPPLIES NEEDED:
Pen
Paper

ESTIMATED TIME:
5 to 10 minutes

This one gives you a chance to make faces at each other in the most grown-up way possible. Bonus points if you play this in public.

INSTRUCTIONS

1. One person expresses an emotion or mood by making a face at their partner.

2. The partner then has to guess the emotion. You can start with descriptors like mad, sad, happy, etc., but try to branch out from there so you can keep the game going.

3. Keep score by writing down the emotion guessed and give yourself 1 point if you guessed correctly, 0 points if guessed incorrectly.

4. It can be more fun if you're trying to guess something a bit obscure. Try these to get you started:

Gleeful/Joyful	Mischievous	Disbelieving	Annoyed
Grieving	Surprised/ Shocked	Hurt	Exasperated
Panicked	Calm/Relaxed	Awestruck	Chipper/Perky
Disgusted	Neutral	Infatuated	Discouraged
Loving	Appalled	Mesmerized	Radiant

5. Tally the score and see who is better at reading faces.

Name: _____   Name: _____

Points	Emotion	Points	Emotion
_____	_____	_____	_____
_____	_____	_____	_____
_____	_____	_____	_____
_____	_____	_____	_____
_____	_____	_____	_____
_____	_____	_____	_____
_____	_____	_____	_____
_____	_____	_____	_____
_____	_____	_____	_____
_____	_____	_____	_____
_____	**Total points**	_____	**Total points**

CHAPTER TWO

Smart

Want to upgrade your status to power couple? Learning how to solve problems as a team will help elevate your brainpower together and highlight how your individual strengths and weaknesses complement each other. If you're ready to exercise your brains and work together, learn a few phrases in a new language, or invent something new, this is your chapter. While some of these activities will take 30 minutes or less, you'll find a few that are perfect for when you've got a few uninterrupted hours together.

The Crossword of Love

 SUPPLIES NEEDED:
Pencil
Timer (optional)

ESTIMATED TIME: 10 minutes

This simple crossword puzzle is all about the frills of love and romance. To add an extra layer of challenge, use a timer to see how quickly you can complete it together.

Across

1. A relationship between two people who are falling in love

2. Roses are _____

3. One way to meet someone special

4. What you do when you're interested in someone

5. (Hopefully) the answer to a marriage proposal

6. _____ upon a time

7. What Cupid does with his bow and arrow

Down

1. How couples get to know each other

2. A sweet treat that makes a good gift

3. What you have for each other (plural)

4. One immediate response you might have when you see your partner

5. To snuggle up together

Answers on page 133

DIY Escape Room

 SUPPLIES NEEDED:
2 rooms with places to hide clues
Paper
Pens
2 keys
Timer

ESTIMATED TIME: 1 to 1½ hours, including setup

Are you ready for a battle of wit and creativity to see who can escape a place first? This activity will give you the opportunity to see how each other's mind works. Observe the types of clues they leave, and find out how quickly you can solve each other's creative puzzles.

INSTRUCTIONS

1. You and your partner will be creating an escape room for the other. Choose two rooms and decide who will design the puzzle for each room. Decide how much time you both get on the timer. Inspect the rooms you'll be using to get ideas for writing clues and puzzles and where to hide them.

2. Have each person make a trail from one clue to the next with riddles, codes (don't forget to make the key for them to find and decode it), word scrambles, and fill-in-the-blank rhymes. The last clue leads to the hidden key, which is proof that the person completed the puzzle.

3. Once your rooms are set up and the first clues are laid out in the open (even if they're not 100 percent obvious), switch rooms, start the timer, and get going. Whoever finds their key first is crowned the winner!

Here's an abbreviated example to get you started. Check the resources (see page 134) for more ideas.

- Your partner sees a note taped to the door that says, "Your next clue will be found where we heard the waves pound." The next clue is taped to the back of a photo of the two of you on the beach.

- That clue contains a coded message with a key to decipher it. You could create your own symbols or use a number for each letter. So "TOOTH FAIRY" (which prompts your partner to check under a pillow) could be 20 15 15 20 8 6 1 9 18 25, which is the numeric order the individual letters appear in the alphabet.

- The clue under the pillow says, "Open it up and you may find . . . something to cover your/my cute behind!" If this is the last clue (use more than three clues if you can), the key is hidden in the underwear drawer, and it's time for them to open the door and stop the timer.

Starts With . . .

SUPPLIES NEEDED:
26 small scraps of paper
Jar or bowl
Pencil or pen
Copy machine
Timer

ESTIMATED TIME: 10 to 15 minutes

It's time to brainstorm and learn just how different your minds are!
You'll be amazed at how your word choices can vary.

INSTRUCTIONS

1. On each of the 26 scraps of paper, write one letter of the alphabet.
   Fold up the scraps of paper and put in them a jar or bowl. Make sure
   you can't see what's written on them from the outside (a pencil is
   best unless the paper type is heavy).

2. Make one to two copies of the following game card with a copy
   machine, or write out the corresponding numbers below to record
   your answers.

3. Reach in and pull one letter out, then set the timer for 1 minute.

4. Using only words that start with that letter, you'll both write down
   one answer to each of the following categories, or as many as you
   can in 1 minute.

TIP: If you each have your own book, you can write on the lines on the
opposite page. If you're together in person and only have one book, pull
out at least one piece of paper and jot the categories down on it.

5. See how many you can get that aren't the same as what your partner
   wrote down. Do you basically share a brain or were your ideas pretty
   different?

1

A person's name:

_____

2

An animal:

_____

3

Something you
might find outside:

_____

4

Something your
significant
other loves:

_____

5

Something your
significant other
doesn't like:

_____

6

Date idea:

_____

7

A place to go:

_____

8

Food:

_____

9

A device:

_____

10

Drink:

_____

11

The title of
a love song:

_____

12

Thing you say
to someone you
like or love:

_____

13

Something
you'll never do:

_____

14

Something
you think your
significant other
would never do:

_____

15

Somewhere you sit:

_____

16

Something that
makes a good gift:

_____

17

A method of
communication:

_____

18

A mode of
transportation:

_____

International Love Languages

SUPPLIES NEEDED:
Device with internet connection

ESTIMATED TIME: 2 to 45 minutes, depending on how many you learn and practice per day

Learn to say "I love you" in 30 languages to stretch your brains and add a little spice to the phrase. This is a great sit-down activity at home or in a restaurant, or as a short part of your daily routine together. It only takes a few minutes a day to learn a new way to say "I love you."

INSTRUCTIONS

1. Using a website or app, look up, "How to say I love you in 30 languages." Check the resources (see page 134) for translator recommendations.

2. Work your way through the list or lists you find.

3. You could also look up the phrase in specific languages with an online translator in your browser or in an app on your phone.

4. Learn how to embellish the phrase any way you'd like. Maybe you want to say, "I love you more every day" or "I will love you forever." Maybe you also want to know how to say "I like you!" If you've been together for a long time, there's a good chance you have your own special phrase to declare your love for each other. Give those a whirl in a translator and see how it goes.

Getting Inventive

 SUPPLIES NEEDED:
Pen
Paper

ESTIMATED TIME: 1 to 1½ hours

What would it be like to invent something new together? Maybe there's something you both wish existed that would solve a problem in your lives or for the world at large. Or perhaps there's something completely frivolous and funny that you'd like to see on the shelves of a store. Teamwork and a whole lot of imagination come together to make this a fun project that can allow you to work together to create something totally unusual and new. See how your strengths and weaknesses balance each other out. Who knows, maybe you'll go into business together after this!

INSTRUCTIONS

1. Sketch your design. If there's packaging and a logo, what does it look like?

2. Envision your target audience. How would you reach them and promote this new product?

3. Decide on a slogan. Make up a jingle for it—bonus points if it rhymes. (Have fun with it!)

4. If you're feeling especially crafty and adventurous (and depending on what you and your significant other have invented), take this activity to the next level and see if you can build a basic model of it.

Conversational

If you have some time but don't have access to many materials other than a pen and paper, you'll love this chapter. Maybe you're out on a date, on a trip, or in a car driving somewhere together. You can use this chapter to get to know each other even better or spark a new conversation—even if you've gotten used to welcoming silence while sitting together. Take the opportunity to add an interesting twist to your day. Be open to seeing where the conversations take you.

Build a New Story

SUPPLIES NEEDED:
Book or internet connection
Pen
Paper (if you need more than this space provides)

ESTIMATED TIME: 10 to 30 minutes

This activity calls for you to combine two separate stories or songs you love to create an entirely new story altogether. Approach this as a fun way to blend two of your interests and get to talking about them. You may even create a brand-new hobby you can regularly do together.

INSTRUCTIONS

1. Grab your favorite books, look up the lyrics to each of your favorite songs, or look up favorite lines from movies.

2. Share your favorite lines with each other and decide which one should be the beginning of a new story and which one should be the end.

3. Write the beginning line below and take turns adding your own sentences, with the goal of getting to the other person's quote.

4. Go on for as long as you'd like, creating twists and turns in the story, or keep it short and sweet. The goal isn't to have a story that makes complete sense, but rather to enjoy weaving a story together.

5. Read it aloud together when you're done.

_____

_____

_____

_____

_____

_____

What Would You Choose?

 ESTIMATED TIME: 15+ minutes

Get to know your significant other better while coming up with serious and absurd scenarios that involve choosing between two things. You may have played something similar before, since this kind of game is often used as an icebreaker at parties and small gatherings. You can write questions ahead of time, but you may find it easier to let yourself get caught up in the moment of playing and let questions come spontaneously as you banter.

INSTRUCTIONS

1. Take turns giving each other a choice between any two things. It could be anything, like general preferences or wacky situations they'd probably never find themselves in. Here are a few examples to get you started:

    -   Mornings or evenings?

    -   Dancing or skipping everywhere you go (instead of walking) or singing every time words come out of your mouth?

    -   To never be able to wear socks again or never eat your favorite food again?

    -   Massage or cuddle?

    -   Square or circle?

    -   To have an iguana attached to your arm for a week or give up your phone for a month?

2. As they answer, feel free to ask about their decision-making process to gain insight into how your partner's mind works.

3. Switch it up, add your own questions, and keep taking turns for as long as you like!

Poetic Conversation

 ESTIMATED TIME: Varies

Poetry is quite a traditional way to express love for a significant other. It may not be for everyone, but you can make it a fun, interactive experience if you commit to only speaking in verse while you spend time together. Want to add a musical and/or updated twist? Try to rap lines instead of just speaking them.

INSTRUCTIONS

1. Choose a set amount of time to spend only speaking to each other in lines of poetry or rap lyrics. Alternatively, you could just start. Wing it and go until you just can't do it anymore.

2. Once you get started, you'll have to speak to each other only in lines of verse, no exceptions! Technically, you could do free verse and take it easy on yourselves, but challenge yourselves to speak in couplets (every two lines rhyme, in an AABB pattern), haikus (five syllables in the first line, seven in the second, and five in the last), or stick to another rhyme scheme of your choice.

Haiku Example:

Would you like to watch

Our favorite TV show?

I will turn it on.

Couplet Example:

Come dance with me in the kitchen, my sweet;

Then I will make us some dinner to eat!

Tell Them How You Really Feel

 SUPPLIES NEEDED:
Paper and pen (optional)

ESTIMATED TIME: 15 minutes

It's easy to miss out on expressing how much you care for, admire, or love your partner for a number of reasons, even when you're in a solid relationship that is full of lighthearted moments and genuine affection for each other. Maybe you're in a new relationship and feeling too shy about freely expressing yourself. Or perhaps your relationship is many decades old and you just assume they *know* how you feel—and you don't need to say anything. Here's a game that will get you both talking, challenging you to come up with and comment on the things you like or love about your significant other and letting them know how you really feel.

INSTRUCTIONS

1. Out loud or on a piece of paper, each partner should list 5 to 10 things they like, love, or admire about the other person.

Begin by completing these statements.

I like/love it when you _____

I like/love you because _____

I appreciate _____

One of the things I admire about you is _____

I get butterflies when you _____

Now, the other partner takes a turn.

I like/love it when you _____

I like/love you because _____

I appreciate _____

One of the things I admire about you is _____

I get butterflies when you _____

2. Write down your own statements, listing what you like, love, or admire about your partner.

_____

_____

_____

_____

_____

_____

_____

_____

_____

Pop Quiz

 SUPPLIES NEEDED:
Pen (optional)

ESTIMATED TIME: 20 minutes

This game will help you get to know each other on a deeper level in a lighthearted way. You can easily do this one over the phone or via video chat.

INSTRUCTIONS

Take turns asking each other these questions, then feel free to add your own questions to the end. You can also mentally quiz yourself to see how well you know your partner as you go.

If you could live in any book, movie, or television show, what would it be?

_____

_____

What's your favorite decade?

_____

_____

What's your favorite childhood memory?

_____

_____

Did you like school when you were a kid? Why?

_____

_____

What's the main thing you want to accomplish by the end of your life?

_____

_____

Are you a dog or cat person?

_____

_____

If you could live anywhere in the world, where would it be (and why)?

_____

_____

When you were a kid, what did you want to be when you grew up?

_____

_____

What's your favorite word?

_____

_____

What's your worst nightmare?

_____

_____

What's your most embarrassing moment? How did you handle it?

_____

_____

If you had to choose a "uniform" (down to specific style and color) to wear for the rest of your life, what would it be?

_____

_____

If you had a theme song for your life, what would it be?

_____

_____

What's your favorite board game?

_____

_____

If you had to watch one show or movie every time you turned the television on for the next five years, what would it be?

_____

_____

What's your favorite tradition (could be something you do with your significant other, friends, family, or alone)?

_____

_____

CHAPTER FOUR

Flirty

One piece of relationship advice I always offer is to never stop flirting with your partner—it keeps things fresh and exciting! Use compliments, touch, sweet messages, and everyday situations as an opportunity to let your significant other know that you find them irresistible. Some of these activities are quick and suitable for every day, while others will take a bit more time to complete. No matter which you choose, these are meant for when you're both feeling a little flirtatious.

We're Superheroes Now

SUPPLIES NEEDED:
Pen or pencil
Markers, crayons, or colored pencils (optional)

ESTIMATED TIME: 10 to 20 minutes

Use this activity to become a superhero duo! Create alter egos for each other that play up your strengths and the things you admire about each other. Use this opportunity to give sly compliments, celebrate the little things and meaningful qualities you love about each other, and add a little absurdity to the mix for laughs.

INSTRUCTIONS

Take turns answering the questions below for your partner.

Name of superhero #1:

_____

What does my costume look like?

_____

What are my superpowers?

_____

What's my Achilles' heel?

_____

What's my strength? (can be more than one)

_____

Pretend we met while in superhero form. What was it about me that you fell for? What do you like/love most about me?

_____

Name of superhero #2:

_____

What does my costume look like?

_____

What are my superpowers?

_____

What's my Achilles' heel?

_____

What's my strength? (can be more than one)

_____

Pretend we met while in superhero form. What was it about me that you fell for? What do you like/love most about me?

_____

How do I transition from my
regular self to my alter ego
and back again?

_____

Do I have a special saying or quirky
habit exclusive to my alter ego?

_____

Where did my powers come from?

_____

We always fight crime together.
Who is our archnemesis and what
does he or she do to wreak havoc?

_____

What do we do to wind down or
celebrate after successfully thwart-
ing our archnemesis's plans?

_____

What makes us such a good team?

_____

Draw a picture of me in
superhero form:

How do I transition from my
regular self to my alter ego
and back again?

_____

Do I have a special saying or quirky
habit exclusive to my alter ego?

_____

Where did my powers come from?

_____

We always fight crime together.
Who is our archnemesis and what
does he or she do to wreak havoc?

_____

What do we do to wind down or
celebrate after successfully thwart-
ing our archnemesis's plans?

_____

What makes us such a good team?

_____

Draw a picture of me in
superhero form:

Invisible Messages

 SUPPLIES NEEDED:
Pen
Sheet of paper (optional)
Tape (optional)

ESTIMATED TIME: 10 minutes

In this activity, you'll write your partner a sweet or funny message using touch rather than sight to find out if they can decipher it. You'll be paying very close attention to each other in this game! If any touch from them sends delightful shivers up your spine, this is definitely the game for you.

INSTRUCTIONS

1. Have your partner either sit or stand facing away from you with their back exposed. Your partner can use this page to write down the message or tape a sheet of paper to the wall in front of them.

2. Using one finger, write a message (a sweet nothing, something funny, etc.) on your partner's back, one letter at a time. Try to write large letters since that will be easier for them to decipher.

3. Have your partner write down each letter they feel on their back.

4. Tell them when you're finished writing and let your partner read the message to see if it's correct.

5. Switch places and do it again. Who was able to decipher a message from their partner?

DIY Spa Day

 SUPPLIES NEEDED:
Fruit and/or herbs
Pitcher of water
Robes (or loungewear)
Relaxing music or
nature sounds

ESTIMATED TIME:
3 hours (including prep)

OPTIONAL BUT RECOMMENDED:
Ingredients for DIY face
masks appropriate for your
skin type
Candles or essential oils and
diffuser
Massage oil
Snacks

Spend some pampering time together in total relaxation without spending a fortune.

INSTRUCTIONS

1. Set up your spa experience. Lay out the snacks, and cut up the fruit or herbs and add them to a pitcher of water. If you'd like, find recipes for at-home face masks based on both of your skin types and prepare the masks using ingredients you have on hand. Put on your robes or loungewear, take a long, deep breath together, and prepare to do nothing but relax.

2. If you'd like, set the mood with clean-smelling candles or essential oils (scents based on florals, fruits, and herbs are good to use). Play some relaxing music or nature sounds.

3. Start by giving each other massages. It can be neck/shoulders, hand/foot, full body, or any combination. It's up to the two of you—the key is to make sure you're both relaxing.

4. If using, apply your face masks and recline side by side somewhere comfortable, listening to the music or nature sounds and enjoying the aromatherapy. Enjoy the fruit-infused water and snacks together.

5. You can relax for as little or as long of a time as you both need. Feel free to customize and add in other things you both find relaxing. If you both find this useful, discuss making it a regularly scheduled activity.

Hello There, Stranger

 ESTIMATED TIME: 15 to 30 minutes, or as long as you both like

By courting each other, you've already impressed each other at least once in real life. For this activity, "meet" each other for the first time again (this time without the pressure!). Have fun in the moment and see where it takes you. Try this activity while you're out running errands in town, or if you're in a long-distance relationship and looking for a way to spice things up.

INSTRUCTIONS

1. Decide which partner will approach the other before you start. Whether you're in public or talking online, act like you're two strangers who have never met before.

2. If in person, one of you will spot the other and just *have* to say hello or they'd always wonder "what if." Long distance? Pretend you met on a dating app and just took it to text, calls, or video calls. What would you tell each other about your lives if you had just met today?

3. Flirt with each other! Engage in silly banter. Compliment each other the way you would if you'd just met and were trying to win their interest and affection. If you've ever wanted to use a cheesy pickup line, now's your chance.

4. Ask each other out. Set up a future date . . . and make this a real one!

Scrambled Words of Affection

This is a quick and easy little activity you can do almost anywhere, unless one of you is driving. If you each have a copy of the book, you can even do it over the phone when it's time to reconnect from a distance.

INSTRUCTIONS

Work together to unscramble the following words and phrases. The below phrases are things one might say or feel in a happy relationship. Write the letters on the line next to each word or phrase. See how quickly you can decipher them all. *Answers on page 133*

OUY REA HET EBST _____

M'I OS ULKCY _____

GHU EM _____

SISK EM _____

UOY AER OS TCUE _____

NANAW EADT _____

IVEOM GHITN _____

N'TAC ITAW OT ESE OUY GAIAN _____ .

OUY KAME EM OS PYPHA _____

VFOERRE N'TIS NGLO GHENUO _____

VFOATIER NSOEPR _____

VEOL UOY TSLO _____

INSESPHAP _____

TEMUOSLAS _____

LDHO YM ANHD _____

CHAPTER FIVE

Loving

Show your partner how much you love them and treasure the time you get to spend together through dancing, putting a scrapbook together, giving compliments, and recreating romantic movie scenes. In this chapter, there's even an activity to do together that will extend some love to strangers. Most of these activities are somewhat flexible on the amount of time you'll need, and some of them can be broken up into phases and completed over time.

Compliments from Around the World

SUPPLIES NEEDED:
Internet connection and/or
a translator app

ESTIMATED TIME:
5 to 10 minutes

Take a moment to gush about each other's admirable qualities—in other languages. Nothing's off-limits. Take time to really observe each other or say what you've been thinking all along.

INSTRUCTIONS

1. Search for a website or app that will allow you to translate phrases from one language to another one of your choice. Check the resources (see page 134) for translator recommendations. Think about something you'd like to compliment your partner on and type that into the translator. Read it aloud or play it from the website or app.

2. Let your partner guess the compliment.

3. Switch places, receive a compliment from your partner, and try to guess what it is.

4. Who gave the most unique or most thoughtful compliment? Try funny and unexpected compliments and switch up the languages as often as you'd like. You'll both leave the activity feeling lighter, happier, and more appreciated.

5. Try to do this once a week, every morning, or every night and make it a part of your daily routine.

6. Transcribe your favorite compliments, and the language, in the lines below as a reminder of what you love about each other.

French	Vous me donnez envie d'être une meilleure personne.

Do Good in the World, as a Team

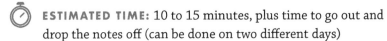

SUPPLIES NEEDED:

Pen or pencil

Sticky notes

Public places to visit

ESTIMATED TIME: 10 to 15 minutes, plus time to go out and drop the notes off (can be done on two different days)

Here's a way to work together and spread a little cheer around to others. Remember that just being with the one you love is a gift. Take the love you feel for each other and extend some of it out into the world.

INSTRUCTIONS

1. Sit down together and write inspiring, funny, and uplifting messages on the sticky notes.

2. Include drawings, if you'd like, and keep the messages pretty general (since you never know who will find them).

3. Once you have a little collection of messages, leave them in unexpected places around your community—like a mirror in a public bathroom, on a bench at the bus stop, or tucked inside a library book—for people to find. You never know whose day you will make brighter.

Ideas for messages to get you started:

"You're amazing!"

"Everything's going to be okay."

"You are loved."

"Have a wonderful day!"

"I'm so grateful the world has YOU in it."

Create a Scrapbook Together

✎ **SUPPLIES NEEDED:**

Scrapbook or blank journal

Tape

Glue

Pens

Markers

Photos, ticket stubs, and miscellaneous objects you've saved
that represent your relationship and will fit inside the pages of
a journal

⏱ **ESTIMATED TIME:** 1 to 1½ hours

Gather all your mementos and supplies and settle in for a trip down memory lane to celebrate the path of your relationship. No matter how long you've been together, you'll find yourself happily reminiscing about shared experiences and the growth that has occurred since you first met. In the process, you'll create a keepsake to reflect on for years to come.

INSTRUCTIONS

1. Use the space on the next page to organize your memories or jot down ideas together. Do you want to go in chronological order? Do you want to organize by theme (movies, concerts, favorite moments, etc.)?

2. Decide which objects belong together and what your layout will be before taping or gluing things down in your scrapbook. Write down short captions or notes about the occasion or theme celebrated on each page.

3. Once you're done, you'll have a special keepsake that you can keep adding to as your relationship grows and deepens.

TIP: If you're not the sentimental type and don't have a lot of ticket stubs and similar items saved up, brainstorm first and draw pictures or write words in their place. This is your art project, so there aren't any rules.

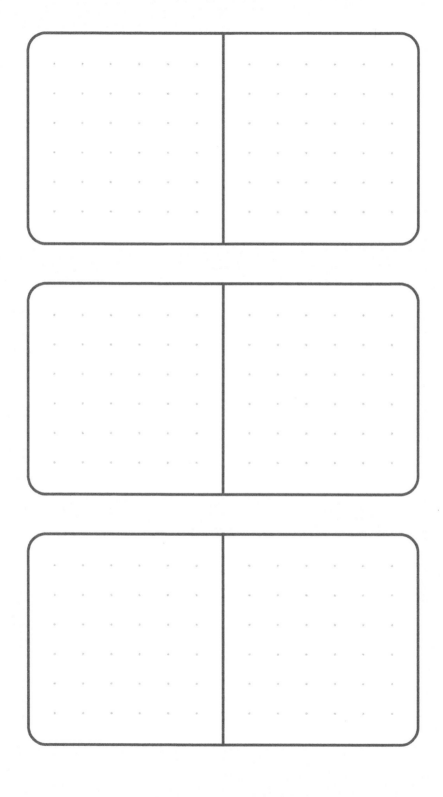

Act Out a Romantic Scene

SUPPLIES NEEDED:
Notecards (optional)
Pen or pencil (optional)
Timer

ESTIMATED TIME: 20 to 30 minutes for a few rounds

If you're a couple of movie buffs or are pretty familiar with romantic comedies, you'll love this charades-inspired activity. Put on your acting hat and give it a try!

INSTRUCTIONS

1. Prepare by brainstorming romantic movie scenes together and writing the movies down in the space provided on the next page or on notecards. Be sure to make several cards to choose from or it'll make the game too easy.

2. Decide who will go first. That partner either chooses a card from the stack, mentally chooses one from the written list on the next page, or thinks of a romantic scene on their own.

3. Set the timer for 30 seconds as soon as the first player starts acting out the movie scene they've chosen. Try to recite lines that will help your partner recall the specific film.

4. When time's up, add another 30 seconds on the timer. Have the other partner jump in to continue acting out the scene *they* think is on the card (or in their significant other's mind).

5. When the timer goes off, reveal the name of the movie.

6. Here are a few movie ideas. Feel free to write in your own!

Casablanca	*Dirty Dancing*
When Harry Met Sally	*Titanic*
Pride & Prejudice	*The Notebook*
Love Actually	*Brokeback Mountain*
Jerry Maguire	*My Best Friend's Wedding*
Sleepless in Seattle	*Ghost*

_____

_____

_____

_____

_____

_____

_____

_____

_____

Get Your Dancing Shoes On

🖎 **SUPPLIES NEEDED:**
Internet connection
Props you may need for your dance of choice

⏱ **ESTIMATED TIME:** 30 minutes to 1 hour

Have you ever wanted to learn how to salsa, line dance, swing dance, waltz, or do some other dance together? Now is the time! You can learn the steps to many dances using an online tutorial (see resources, page 134). You will likely need more than one lesson, so keep this activity in your regular rotation to master a dance. Then you'll be confident to try it out in public later.

INSTRUCTIONS

1. Decide which dance you should learn together. Should it be fast-paced or slow? Modern or old-timey? The sky's the limit.

2. Find classes for that dance online and get ready to learn. There are tons of resources to learn for free, but there are paid options, too.

3. If you happen to have things lying around the house that could make practice more fun (like a fun, flouncy dress or some heels that would be perfect for learning to salsa), put those into action!

4. Keep a list of the steps you're learning here so you can remind yourselves of all the moves (not just the ones you remember off the tops of your heads). You'll eventually be able to practice them without watching a video.

_____

_____

_____

_____

Nostalgic

Escape to another time or place (or both!) with your significant other. Go on a date from another decade, or relive some of the favorite parts of your childhoods and take them along for the ride. Express yourself in an old-school love letter to be tucked away and reread time and time again. You could also choose to revisit the memories you've made recently and then save some for later in a time capsule. No matter your activity choice, let your love be one for the ages.

Time Travelers

If you've ever wished you had lived and met each other in a different era, now is the time to pretend that you did. Everything from the clothes that you wear and the music you may listen to, to the meal that you eat and the way that you talk, is up to you to enact.

INSTRUCTIONS

1. Think back in history and pick a time period from the past that is meaningful or interesting to both of you.

2. Research the food, clothing, and social or romantic customs of that era. Find and make a recipe you think you'll enjoy preparing and eating together. You can go as traditional or out-there by today's standards as you would like. Feel free to add extra courses, such as appetizers, desserts, or even drinks that harken back to that time.

3. When the food is ready, enjoy it together by candlelight with some music from that era (if applicable). Decide whether or not you'll dress up in clothes from the era to take it to the next level!

4. Depending on the time period, you may want to follow the meal up with a book, game, or traditional activity from the past era you've chosen.

Write Love Letters

 SUPPLIES NEEDED:

Paper

Pen

Envelope

ESTIMATED TIME: 30 minutes

There's something so special about a handwritten love note. Whether you live under the same roof or hundreds or thousands of miles away from each other, this activity will prompt you to open up and pour your feelings onto paper.

INSTRUCTIONS

1. Choose your paper and pen. Maybe you want to try a fountain pen and formal or heavyweight paper for the occasion, but don't feel obligated to go to that extreme. Any pen and a sheet of paper will work; the most important thing is to get your true feelings across to your significant other.

2. Once you've gathered your supplies, sit down with absolutely no distractions and write your partner an old-fashioned love letter. Reflect on their best qualities, what they mean to you, and what you wish to tell them. Don't hold back on your thoughts, feelings, and the flourishes of your pen.

3. Seal the letter up and write your partner's name on the envelope. Decide whether you'll open each other's letter now or wait until a designated time to read them.

4. Swap letters in person, or drop them in the mail.

Dating in the Decades Past

⌦ **SUPPLIES NEEDED:**

Internet connection

Decade-appropriate clothing (optional)

Decade-appropriate board game or movie (optional)

⏱ **ESTIMATED TIME:** 2+ hours

Enjoy a break from modern life by choosing a decade of the recent past and planning a date you could have only taken at that time. You may have to mix a little old and new, depending on what you decide to do, but it'll still be a delightful, almost time-traveling adventure.

INSTRUCTIONS

1. Go online and look for typical dates for different decades you're interested in.

2. See if you two can piece outfits together that are throwbacks to the decade you've chosen. You don't have to spend a lot; get creative with what's in your closets and what you can find at a thrift store.

3. Plan your date here and sketch the outfit you'd like to wear.

Some ideas:

- Find a local jazz club with a 1920s vibe (or create that vibe at home).

- Love the idea of a date from the 1950s? Stop off for a milkshake with two straws and drive around listening to doo-wop, rock and roll, or the blues. (If there's a drive-in movie theater in or near your town, you *have* to make that part of the experience.)

- Slip into a pair of bell-bottoms and dance the night away with a disco night—in a club or at home!

- Put on your flannel shirt, slip dress, or bucket hat. Turn on some music from the 1990s and drive to the mall. Walk around for hours and eat at a chain restaurant, then meet up with a group of friends or go home to watch a '90s blockbuster.

TIP: You could even pair this one with the previous online dance lessons activity. Simply choose a decade-appropriate dance to end your evening or try learning a few steps while dinner is cooking.

What We'll Do: _____

_____

_____

What We'll Wear:

Revisit Your Childhood

 SUPPLIES NEEDED:

Various candy and snacks you enjoyed as a kid

Old movies or TV shows you used to enjoy

Board games from your childhood decade

Video games you used to play (optional)

ESTIMATED TIME: 3+ hours

Do you miss the sugar-laden, carefree days of childhood? It's not often that our adult partners were part of our childhood years. Now's the time to take a trip to some of your favorite memories from the past—with your significant other! If you and your significant other grew up in different decades or enjoyed different games growing up, you can do this activity twice—once for each of your childhoods.

INSTRUCTIONS

1. Make lists of your favorite candy, snacks, movies, and activities you loved as kids.

2. Buy the candy and snacks you're able to find. Check a streaming service or buy a digital version of a few of your favorite movies or shows.

3. If you're not in the mood to watch something, pull out some old board games or connect an old console to your TV to play some video games.

4. Spend the night playing together and remembering what it was like to be kids.

TIP: Was your collection tossed out a long time ago? Check thrift stores to see if they have old board games. Many classic video games are now available digitally if you no longer have the console or game cartridges to play. If you're hoping to play a game of Twister, there are even game spinner apps so you can play without a third person to spin the wheel.

Candy and Snacks

Movies and Activities

_____   _____

_____   _____

_____   _____

_____   _____

_____   _____

_____   _____

_____   _____

_____   _____

_____   _____

_____   _____

_____   _____

_____   _____

_____   _____

Make a Time Capsule

Sealable plastic bag

Airtight, waterproof
container or archival box

Epoxy glue (if burying the
time capsule)

Waterproof label

Shovel (if burying the
capsule outside)

Safe place to hide the
time capsule

A way to mark where
you've put it

ESTIMATED TIME: 1 hour

Take a walk down memory lane and create a keepsake so you can reminisce in the future! Save some of your favorite memories for later, in physical form, that remind you of each other and the time you've spent together. You'll also agree on a future date to open the capsule and laugh and reflect at what you've captured at this moment in time.

INSTRUCTIONS

1. Together, discuss and gather objects that remind you of important moments in your relationship. What little objects have you held on to that would be fun to look back on someday? Be sure to toss in a few things that represent the present day for fun and for historical context. Don't bury anything especially sentimental; make copies or take photos and add those instead, just in case you can't access the container later or water somehow gets in. Consult the resources (see page 134) for more tips on preparing a time capsule.

2. Arrange your items in the sealable plastic bag, place them inside the container, seal it with the epoxy glue, label it, bury it somewhere safe, and mark the spot on a map if you want to go the traditional time capsule route. If you feel more comfortable keeping it indoors, you can use an archival box hidden at the back of a closet or in the attic to keep things safe from the outdoors.

3. Choose a date in the future that you will open the time capsule, if you like. You can even send yourself a reminder to open it using FutureMe.org or a calendar app.

Imaginative

Where could your minds take you today? It could be an indoor camping trip or a plan for your perfect vacation. You could become different people, find a new use for an old object, or simply work on a messy art project together. The sky is the limit, whether you're enjoying an evening in or a night out. Exercising your creativity as a couple will train you to always be on the lookout for ways to make each other feel special, seek out new experiences (or new twists on old ones), and help your relationship evolve and thrive.

Go Camping . . . Indoors!

 SUPPLIES NEEDED:

Sleeping bags (optional)

Glow-in-the-dark stars

Favorite music or nature sounds

Ghost stories to share (you could make them up on the fly, find
them online, or grab a book and a flashlight)

Microwave

Chocolate bar

Jumbo marshmallows

Graham crackers

ESTIMATED TIME: 2 hours to most (or all) of the night

Take this opportunity to recreate the fun of a night spent in the great
outdoors—without leaving your living room! While some things may
require a device, try to keep this experience as distraction-free as possible—just as if you'd set up a tent in the middle of the woods.

INSTRUCTIONS

1. Set up your sleeping bags, if you're using them.

2. Place the glow-in-the-dark stars on the ceiling.

3. Find a playlist of your favorite songs or really add to the outdoor
   camping experience with a playlist of nature sounds.

4. Turn off the lights and snuggle up with your special someone.

5. Listen to the sounds of nature or your favorite tunes, tell some
   ghost stories, and pop out to the "campfire" (aka the microwave) to
   make s'mores. See where the conversation takes you as you gaze up
   at the stars.

Mixed Media Portraits

SUPPLIES NEEDED:

Tarp

Scraps of fabric and
   anything else you might
   want for a mixed media art
   project (this one's really up
   to you!)

Canvas or other base for
   your masterpiece

Markers

Paint

Paintbrushes

Glue

Old magazines and
   newspapers

Pencils

Pens

Scissors

Blindfold(s)

ESTIMATED TIME: 1 to 1½ hours

How do you *really* see each other? Use whatever you have on hand at home to create mixed media portraits of one another while wearing blindfolds. You can choose a combination of ink, paint, colored pencils, cloth, paper, beads, and any other art supplies you have on hand—the sky's the limit! This one is sure to get some laughs both during and after the activity.

INSTRUCTIONS

1. First, prep both of your work areas: Lay the tarp down, arrange all your gathered items somewhere within reach, and set up the canvases for your creation. If you want to use cutouts from magazines or newspapers, go ahead and cut those out.

2. Put on the blindfolds. Use what's there to create mixed media portraits of each other while blindfolded.

3. Check out your masterpieces and have a good laugh once the blindfolds come off.

TIP: Decide if you want to take your chances with both of you being blindfolded at the same time. If not, you can take turns and help each other out and avoid making *too* much of a mess. You can also choose to omit the blindfolds altogether, if you prefer.

Plan Your Dream Vacation

 SUPPLIES NEEDED:

Pen or pencil

Paper (optional)

Internet connection

Candles (optional)

A device to play background sounds (optional)

ESTIMATED TIME: 30 minutes to 1 hour

Have a relaxing evening by taking some time to fantasize about your perfect getaway with your partner. Don't let the thought of costs or money limit you—whisk each other away to new places. You could visit a tropical island and tour Europe in the same night. Let yourself get carried away by your wildest travel dreams.

INSTRUCTIONS

1. Brainstorm and create an itinerary. Imagine what you'll see (doodle it on your itinerary!), how you'll feel, what the weather will be like, what you'll eat, what you'll wear, and what you'll shop for.

2. Set the mood with scented candles if you have any that fit the vibe of the vacation you're planning. Play some of the sounds you'd hear if you were there, like waves crashing against the shore, the ambient sounds of a coffee shop, or forest sounds.

3. Close your eyes and walk through your trip together, keeping the itinerary handy to guide you through your imaginary getaway. Save it in case you need ideas for the real thing later.

TIP: Use Google Earth to virtually visit the places on your list.

OUR TRAVEL ITINERARY

SIGHTSEEING STOPS

SHOPPING LIST

RESTAURANTS

Get New Identities

⟋ SUPPLIES NEEDED:
Props or costume (optional)
Pen or pencil (optional)

⏱ ESTIMATED TIME:
1 to 1½ hours or more

Spice things up by becoming a totally different couple for a bit of time or two strangers. You're not remeeting each other here—you're reinventing your lives entirely. It's up to you! Brush up on your acting skills together and see each other in a brand-new way. Where will your imaginations take you?

INSTRUCTIONS

1. Pretend you're celebrities, historical figures, or characters from your favorite fictional books or movies. You don't have to choose people who are (or have been) in a relationship, so famous couples and romance aren't required. Maybe Elizabeth Bennet could meet Abraham Lincoln. How would that conversation go? No one is off-limits.

2. Go on a date, run errands together, or spend time at home, but only communicate with each other as your characters. This will open the door to some interesting (and potentially hilarious) conversations.

TIP: If you end up doing this activity more than once, take notes each time you do it. You may end up with a notebook full of zany, amusing stories to share or enjoy together years from now.

No costumes? Draw what you imagine yourselves to be wearing here:

The Unconventional Side of Things

 SUPPLIES NEEDED:
Any object you'd like to use
Pen or pencil
Paper (if you want to do this more than once)

ESTIMATED TIME: 15 to 20 minutes

Team up for this activity and let your imaginations soar together so you can see the potential for new uses of everyday objects. While this is mostly an exercise in ingenuity for the sake of pure fun, this could also be a helpful exercise if you're trying to transition to a minimalist lifestyle. Either way, this is a way to get creative with almost no planning, and you can do it anywhere. If you're in a long-distance relationship, you can still do this one together over the phone or video chat.

INSTRUCTIONS

1. Choose a random object in your house or something that just happens to be in front of you if you're not at home. If you're out shopping, choose something inexpensive to buy and then bring it home. If you're driving around, it could be something you think up in the moment, rather than something you actually see.

2. How else could this item be used? Brainstorm unconventional uses for it. If you'd like to take it further, try some of your theories to see if they would really work (with caution, of course!).

Object: _____

What it can be or do: _____

_____

Object: _____

What it can be or do: _____

_____

CHAPTER EIGHT

Adventurous

Do you and your partner ever feel stuck in a rut? The weight of a routine or feeling that you just can't seem to break out of everyday tasks can put a damper on any relationship or individual. It's time for an adventure! This is the moment to shake things up! Taste new foods, experience more of the world, learn a new hobby, see your regular roads or trails through new eyes, or make a new four-legged friend. Make a pact to stay open to new adventures and you'll strengthen your bond while creating wonderful memories to look back on later.

Eating Around the World, Tapas-Style

Cookbooks (see resources, page 134)

Internet access

Recipe ingredients (varies by recipe)

Tools you'll need for preparation and cooking (varies by recipe)

🕐 **ESTIMATED TIME:** 3+ hours, excluding planning and shopping

If you want to be world travelers but can't make it happen right now, try sampling recipes from different areas of the world and eating them tapas-style. *Tapas* are an appetizer or snack in Spanish cuisine and translates to "small plates." This style of plating means you won't have to commit to one thing for dinner; instead, you can sample several dishes for a range of flavor profiles from around the globe.

INSTRUCTIONS

1. Choose your menu based on what you already have in your kitchen and pantry. Or, plan your menu and then shop for everything you need. Try featuring different parts of the world in your dinner. For example, you could try dishes like tabbouleh, mango lassi, elote, or empanadas. You could each make a list of countries you're most interested in trying the food from, or even try to represent every continent!

2. Preparing multiple dishes (even if they're simple) can be a lot of work for two people, so turn on some music (bonus if it's new or global music) and chat while you prepare to taste your way around the world.

TIP: If making more than one dish in a day is overwhelming, stretch this date across a week and make a signature meal from one country per day. This is a good one to try if you're enjoying a "staycation" because you'll have extra time on your hands.

Scavenger Hunt

 SUPPLIES NEEDED:
Pencil
Walking shoes
Camera (optional)

ESTIMATED TIME: 1 hour

Take some time to stroll through the neighborhood, a park, a nature trail, or even a mall while you explore with your partner. Commit to making this time a distraction-free activity without phones (unless they're for photos) and you'll get to enjoy working together toward a common goal.

INSTRUCTIONS

1. On the lines below, make a list of things you want to challenge your-selves to find or spot during your outing. Make it geared toward the place you're headed and the time of year.

2. Since it's just the two of you, you'll be on the same team and can go through the hunt as quickly or slowly as you'd like. Consider adding things like red sneakers, a deer, a squirrel, a fallen tree limb, a bike, another happy couple, an old sign, a pinecone, a colorful rock, or water.

3. As you find the things on your list, check them off. If you can snap a photo with some of the items, do that so you can use them in scrap-books or just enjoy looking back at the memories on your camera or phone later.

☐ _____   ☐ _____

☐ _____   ☐ _____

☐ _____   ☐ _____

☐ _____   ☐ _____

☐ _____   ☐ _____

Go Make a Dog's Day

 SUPPLIES NEEDED:
> A local dog shelter that will allow you to take dogs out for the day for socialization, exercise, and fun
> Identification

ESTIMATED TIME: Several hours

If you're not ready to (or can't) have a dog of your own, you and your partner can still reap some of the benefits of time with a furry pal. The dogs will appreciate the time away from the shelter, and you'll be able to help tell the shelter more about their personalities so they can be placed in their perfect forever homes.

INSTRUCTIONS

1. Once you've located a shelter that will allow you to spend time with a dog for a day, make your plan. Is there a trail you want to visit? Do you want to take them to a coffee shop for a small cup of whipped cream? Do you have a fenced-in yard or know of a usually deserted dog park where you can play fetch and run around together? Are there dog-friendly breweries and restaurants in your city where you can enjoy each other's company on a sunny patio?

2. Pick up the dog at the shelter, go on your outing, get to know the dog, and bring them back to the shelter when it's time, armed with plenty of information about the dog that the shelter can use for the dog to find a good home.

3. Before saying goodbye, take a picture of the three of you together and tape or glue it here.

I Spy ... Us!

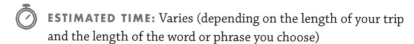

ESTIMATED TIME: Varies (depending on the length of your trip and the length of the word or phrase you choose)

If you're tired of staring out the window on road trips in silence or arguing over the radio station (or just the volume) while you drive, give this game a try. The rules are similar to I Spy, where you find an object that begins with each letter of the word or phrase you choose, but this time you'll take turns spotting things that remind you of each other and your relationship. You can begin at the spur of the moment and repeat it with different words for the length of the trip.

INSTRUCTIONS

1. Choose a word or phrase. If it's a very short trip, choose a short word, and if you'll be driving for hours, choose a phrase to keep you busy a little longer.

2. As you drive, identify objects that remind you of each other in the order of the word or phrase. For example, if your word is hello, you might see a house, eagle, light, leasing office, and officer. Try to guess the significance of the word your partner chose—maybe it's a house that looks like your first home together, the eagle is the mascot of your favorite sports team, etc. See if you can time it just right so that you're on your last letter just as the trip ends.

Hobby Swap

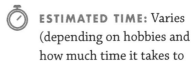 **SUPPLIES NEEDED:**
Supplies you normally use
  for your hobbies
Pen or pencil

ESTIMATED TIME: Varies
(depending on hobbies and
how much time it takes to
get set up and participate)

Get to know each other a little better by getting an inside look at what your partner really likes to do with their free time. Who knows, you may come out of it with the realization that you have a common interest you didn't already know about!

INSTRUCTIONS

1. Each partner should pick one of the other person's personal hobbies to explore for a set amount of time.

2. Gather your materials and be sure to go over any dos and don'ts so your supplies come back to you in good shape.

3. Work side by side, taking time to teach each other as you go. Spend as much time as you need to make sure each of you gets a good taste of what the other person enjoys.

Draw a picture of the finished product here:

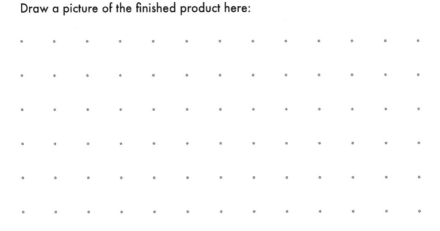

TIP: If your hobbies prohibit you from working side by side, take turns teaching each other about your respective interests. Try them both out and then show each other what you've accomplished.

CHAPTER NINE

Mindful

I s it time to slow things down in life to take things up a notch in your relationship? If so, this chapter is for you. Use the activities that follow to challenge yourselves to stay in the moment and be more observant of yourself and each other. You can revisit this section whenever you and your significant other feel like you need a break from the go-go-go speed of daily life.

What's in the Smoothie?

 SUPPLIES NEEDED:

Smoothie-friendly
  ingredients (fruits, greens,
  coconut water, milk, etc.)
Spices

Ice
Blender
Blindfold (optional)
Pen or pencil

ESTIMATED TIME: 20 minutes

Do you trust each other with your taste buds? Try this activity on a hot day or when you could use a (potentially) healthy snack. No matter the outcome, you'll have fun together in the process.

INSTRUCTIONS

1. Decide how many ingredients you're each allowed to use in the smoothies you're going to make. It doesn't matter if it's three, five, or ten, as long as both smoothies have the same number.

2. One partner makes a smoothie for their blindfolded (or not) significant other. If you don't want to use a blindfold, just make sure the recipient of the smoothie can't see what's going in the blender.

3. Write the ingredients you used on the lines on the next page. Try to be nice and make a smoothie that you think they would enjoy.

4. As they sip the delightful concoction you came up with, have them guess what you put in it. Check them off on the list you made below.

5. Once they're done guessing, switch roles and repeat steps 2 through 5. See who can get the most correct answers.

TIP: Be sure to verify any food allergies with each other before starting.

Smoothie 1

☐ _____

☐ _____

☐ _____

☐ _____

☐ _____

☐ _____

☐ _____

Smoothie 2

☐ _____

☐ _____

☐ _____

☐ _____

☐ _____

☐ _____

☐ _____

Calm Yourselves with Art

 SUPPLIES NEEDED:

Copy machine (optional)
Timer (optional)
Pencil
Paper (lined, graph,
or blank)

Black pen or marker that
won't smear (optional)
Coloring supplies (markers,
crayons, pens, or colored
pencils)

ESTIMATED TIME: 30+ minutes

There are a few different ways to do this activity, depending on how artistic you and your partner feel like being. You can make copies of the design in this book and color them in, or create your own using this one as inspiration.

INSTRUCTIONS

1. Make two copies of the coloring page in this book, if you're planning to color this image.

2. Find a comfortable seat. Settle in so you can feel yourself start to relax. If you have a limited amount of time, set a timer because there's a good chance you could lose track of time while working on this.

3. If you're drawing your own design, sketch out the squares and rectangles first (they can be as big or small as you'd like) on your paper. Then go in and draw a pattern in each square. Trace the squares and patterns with the black pen or marker and then color the designs with your coloring supplies.

4. You can also trade pages after the outlines are done and color each other's designs.

Envisioning More Fun

 SUPPLIES NEEDED:

Old magazines

Catalogs

Scissors

Poster board

Glue

Markers (optional)

ESTIMATED TIME: 45 minutes to 1½ hours

Vision boards are meant to help you plan your life and keep your big goals and dreams at the forefront of your mind. This is not that kind of vision board. Instead, visualize all the little (and big!) things you'd like to do together as a couple, from trying fries dipped in a chocolate shake to dressing up and going to a local play to a scavenger hunt around town to committing to study a new language with each other for 30 days.

INSTRUCTIONS

1. Choose your time frame (a month, six months, a year, five years, etc.).

2. Cut out pictures or words that symbolize things you'd like to do over the course of your time frame.

3. Position the pieces on the poster board to create a collage, but don't glue anything down yet.

4. Once everything looks good, glue it down and fill in white space with words or drawings that represent your relationship or things you want to do together that you couldn't find cutouts for.

5. Hang it up so you'll never run out of date ideas.

Pay Extra Attention

 SUPPLIES NEEDED:
Pencil

ESTIMATED TIME: 2 minutes to 1 hour

How well do you pay attention to each other and the world around you? You're about to find out! You can play this pop quiz anywhere, as long as you're together.

INSTRUCTIONS

1. See how observant your partner is by asking them questions about your environment, other people, or maybe even yourself. If you've been together for a while and questions about each other and your surroundings would be too easy, use a movie or television show as the subject for this game.

2. Take turns asking each other questions. Correct answers get a point and you can keep score with a pencil here.

3. You need to be able to verify an answer without giving your partner a chance to peek. For example, if you ask what color your socks are, hide your feet right before asking. Or, pause the movie and ask what was on the counter behind a certain character, then rewind it to see if they were right.

4. Bookmark this page so you can keep a running tally if you plan to play over an extended period of time. Find out which one of you pays closest attention.

Partner 1:   Partner 2:

_____   _____

Score: Score:

Couple's Meditation Time

 SUPPLIES NEEDED:
Internet access (optional)   Timer
A comfortable place to sit   Pen or pencil

ESTIMATED TIME: 5 to 10 minutes

Can you sit together in silence? Is that the key to a successful relationship? The goal of this activity is just to relax with one another and reset from your day. Try it in the middle of a hectic weekend, before a date night, or when you both get home from work. Or use it to set the tone for a calmer day by spending this quality time together early in the morning.

INSTRUCTIONS

1. If you have internet access, find a short, guided meditation online that is appropriate for your goal. Do you need one that will help you remember to be kind, or are you looking to relax before bed? If you don't want to use a guided meditation, you can just focus on your breath. Check the resources (see page 134) for recommendations on meditation apps and websites.

2. Sit close enough to each other so that you're touching, such as knee-to-knee while you're facing each other in a cross-legged position, or holding hands. Sit up straight and start the meditation recording.

3. If you're not using a guided meditation, set a timer and practice square breathing by exhaling all the air from your lungs. Gently inhale through your nose for a count of four, hold the breath for a count of four, gently exhale the breath for a count of four, and hold the exhale for a count of four. You can either maintain eye contact or close your eyes. Repeat until the timer goes off.

4. Journal about how you feel when you're done. If you're able to turn this into a regular part of your routine, consider starting a dedicated journal to record your feelings during this shared meditation time.

CHAPTER TEN

Truthful

No matter how long you've been together, there are still things you (probably) don't know about each other. Use the activities in this chapter to ask all your burning questions, share more about yourself with each other, and see how well you actually do know each other. Feel free to ask for (or volunteer) more information during or after the activities.

I've Never . . .

SUPPLIES NEEDED:
4 paper plates (optional)
Pen or marker
4 popsicle sticks or similar (optional)
Tape or glue (optional)

ESTIMATED TIME: 10+ minutes, or as long as you want to play

You'll be surprised what you learn about your partner in this game. Get to know each other better and see how well you *already* know each other with this exchange. Hilarity can ensue, so enjoy being silly.

INSTRUCTIONS

1. You could play with verbal responses, but if you'd prefer to have signs, start by prepping your materials. Write "I haven't!" on two plates and "I have!" on the other two. Glue or tape a popsicle stick to the back of each plate to use as handles.

2. Start off with, "I've never . . ." and say something you've never done. The other person then holds up a plate that says they either have or haven't done the thing you named. Take turns naming things you've never done.

3. Feel free to take control and come up with your own situations (stay away from anything that might spark an argument, of course!), but here are a few to get you started.

    Rolled down a hill
    Eaten squid
    Fallen on your face in public
    Gone to a concert
    Peeked at Christmas presents
    Gotten a pedicure
    Purchased something from an infomercial

4. If you do want a way to keep score and have a way to win the game, keep a tally below of how many things each of you has done that the other one has not. The first one to 10 wins.

TIP: You could just name an action, whether you've done it or not, and simultaneously hold up plates to see who has or has not done that thing.

Partner 1:   Partner 2:

_____   _____

Score: Score:

Guess What's in the Box

  SUPPLIES NEEDED:

An item that represents something about you

Box

Pen or pencil

ESTIMATED TIME: 20 to 30 minutes

How well does your partner know you? One partner will choose a mystery item that represents them, and it's up to the other partner to figure out what it is. See how many questions they have to ask before they can figure out what's inside.

INSTRUCTIONS

1. Choose an item that represents you. It could be a hobby, an interest, or something you feel really sums up who you are as a person. Put it in a box and be sure your partner does not see what it is.

2. Have your partner ask you only yes or no questions until they can guess what's in the box. Write the questions below and circle yes or no as you go, so they'll be able to refer back to them as they continue to guess.

   Suggested questions:

   Is this something from childhood?

   Does this have to do with a hobby?

   Is this work related?

   Will I be surprised to see what's in the box?

TIP: If you don't have a box or no longer have a tangible item to use, you can write the word for what you would normally use and tuck it inside an envelope.

_____ Yes No

_____ Yes No

_____ Yes No

_____ Yes No

_____ Yes No

_____ Yes No

_____ Yes No

_____ Yes No

_____ Yes No

_____ Yes No

_____ Yes No

_____ Yes No

_____ Yes No

_____ Yes No

_____ Yes No

_____ Yes No

_____ Yes No

_____ Yes No

_____ Yes No

_____ Yes No

_____ Yes No

_____ Yes No

Tell Me Everything

 ESTIMATED TIME: 5 to 20 minutes

Try interviewing your partner with these 10 questions. How well do you know each other's fears and embarrassments? You may be surprised by some of the answers you get.

INSTRUCTIONS

Take turns asking each other questions from the following list. Feel free to add your own questions at the end, as you like.

What is a silly secret you hide about yourself that you don't mind sharing with me?

What quirky or funny things do you tend to do when you're alone?

What is the theme song for your life?

What is your weirdest fear?

What's the most embarrassing moment you've ever experienced?

If you had to choose a different career than the one you're in (or currently planning), what would it be?

If you had to give up one of your five senses, what would it be and why?

If you could have any pet, what would it be?

If you could be another person for a day, who would you choose?

Which food could you enjoy every single day for the rest of your life?

Seeing the Future

SUPPLIES NEEDED:
Pen or pencil
Paper (optional)

ESTIMATED TIME:
1 to 2 minutes

This is a quick little activity that'll tell you the future and status of your relationship. Phew! Not really. But it's fun to see which words stand out to you both and to ponder their significance together.

INSTRUCTIONS

Take a look at the word search and circle the three to five words you see first. You can do this together or each take a turn. Whatever stands out first describes your relationship now and in the future. Do you and your partner see the same words? If you want to come back and do this activity more than once, write down the words on a separate sheet of paper.
Answers on page 133

I U Y P P A H V P A M T U T
P N T E G I L T E N E U R C
P E T L C U T E L A A E S O
L D R I E E O F O R N P U N
A E O F M U T T V E T G P N
Y R J M E A S N I V T N P E
F O N O T C T D N E O O O C
U M H L Y F T E G R B R R T
L A E A O F U M V O E T T E
R N P F C P U N A F T S I D
V E D G R O S L V T V T V S
L U F T C E P S E R C F E S
O E I L L C G P I T F H E M
O Y F F G N I T S U R T E E

Targeting the Truth

 SUPPLIES NEEDED:

Copy machine

Pen or pencil

Scrap paper

Coin or pebble small enough to toss at the target

ESTIMATED TIME: 15 to 30 minutes

If you're looking for a little competition to get conversation flowing, look no further. The outcome of this game depends on your ability to hit the target, so aim well!

INSTRUCTIONS

1. Make a photocopy of the target to ensure it lays flat during the game. Decide how many rounds you'd like to play.

2. Choose three themes (e.g., childhood stories, favorites, and secrets) together and come up with a few questions for each theme.

3. Write each question on scrap paper, making a separate pile for each theme. Place them facedown.

4. Assign each theme a point value. For example:

   Favorites = 5

   Childhood stories = 7

   Secrets = 10

5. Lay the photocopy down on a flat surface and toss the coin or pebble onto the target. See which section you land on and add that many points to your tally. Pull a question from the corresponding pile and ask your partner to answer it.

6. Then it's your partner's turn. Keep going until you've completed all the rounds. Tally the points at the end to determine the winner.

Here are some questions to get you started.

Favorites:

If you had to eat one type of cuisine for the rest of your life, what would it be?

What are three nonessential things you absolutely need to have in your life?

Childhood Stories:

Who embarrassed you most when you were growing up?

What's one of the defining moments of your childhood that you think played a big part in who you are today?

Secrets:

What's something you've never told me about yourself?

What's something you're afraid of?

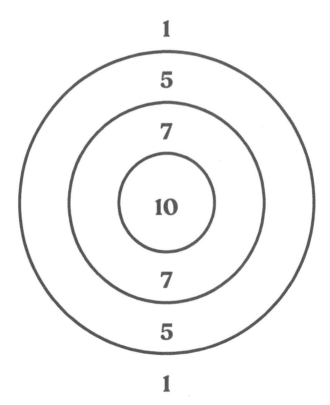

CHAPTER ELEVEN

Daring

This chapter is all about breaking out of your comfort zone and daring to leave some things up to chance. Add a little excitement to your lives by cobbling a date together from random lists, playing a game of Spin the Bottle that can result in anything from a sensual massage to a chore, or challenging yourselves to go out and act ridiculous together in public. The important thing is to delight in each other's company and enjoy the adventure.

DIY Obstacle Course

 SUPPLIES NEEDED:
Pen or pencil
Paper
Timer
Objects for course, such as hard-boiled egg, small ball, spoon,
   items you can step over or weave around, yarn, scarf, and book
   (optional and subject to what you determine you need for your
   obstacle course)

ESTIMATED TIME: 1 to 2 hours

What kinds of obstacles will you overcome for your love? Which one of
you can get through the challenges most quickly? Embrace your inner
child with this one, and make it as silly or exciting as you'd like.

INSTRUCTIONS

1. Chart out and build an obstacle course. This will depend on what
    you have around the house, how much room you have, and what
    your physical limits are. Tailor it based on what suits you best!

    Ideas for an obstacle course:

    - Tightrope walk with yarn or a thin scarf stretched
      across the floor

    - Balancing a hard-boiled egg or ball on a spoon

    - Weaving in and out of a variety of household items

    - Stepping on and over sturdy stools or benches

    - A quick kiss for your partner

    - Signs that give a task to complete (like 10 jumping jacks)

2. Write down the order of the challenges so you both know what to
    do. Make a starting line and finish line and go through the course.
    Time each other to see who can get through it the fastest.

Surprise Drop-Offs

SUPPLIES NEEDED:
Small gift for a friend
Label or note for the gift

ESTIMATED TIME: 5 to 10 minutes, plus drive time

Your love for each other is grand in scale, so why keep it to yourselves? Do something nice for someone together so they can feel loved and special, too. Plus, you'll get the thrill of pulling off a surprise while you're bringing someone a little joy.

INSTRUCTIONS

1. Think of a friend who means something to one or both of you, and brainstorm what you might like to give them as a gift.

2. Wrap the gift you've chosen and attach a note to it that says who it's from and how you were just thinking of them and wanted to brighten their day. Walk or drive over to their home, leave the gift by the door, ring the doorbell (or don't, if they have dogs or small children who might be sleeping), and depart quickly.

3. If you opted not to ring the doorbell, text them something along the lines of "Ding-dong! Surprise at the door" so they'll know to check by the door. (Don't go at night or ring the doorbell when you think they may be asleep for your safety and as a courtesy to your friend.)

Leave It to Chance

 SUPPLIES NEEDED:
Pen or pencil

ESTIMATED TIME: 15 minutes

Plan a date that leaves every choice up to chance. Do you remember playing M.A.S.H. as a kid? It was a giggle-inducing way to see who you were going to marry, where you were going to live, and more. Let's use the rules of M.A.S.H. to plan your next date night.

INSTRUCTIONS

1. Choose which one of you will wield the pen. Fill out the lists below with multiple options for each aspect of your date.

2. Without your partner looking, slowly draw a spiral in the box and have your partner say when to stop. Count the lines of the spiral from one side to the other. Write that number here: _____.

3. Next, use the number from the spiral to eliminate all but one option in each category. Starting with the first category and carrying straight on to the next one (and maybe even the next), count your answers until you land on the number above. Eliminate the option you land on. Continue from there until you hit that number again and eliminate that option. Keep counting and cycling through your options until only one response per category remains. This is your next date!

Type of Food

_____

_____

_____

_____

_____

Music to Enjoy

_____

_____

_____

_____

_____

What to Wear

_____

_____

_____

_____

_____

What to Drink

_____

_____

_____

_____

_____

Activity to Enjoy

_____

_____

_____

_____

_____

Extras (coffee/dessert/etc.)

_____

_____

_____

_____

_____

Spin the Bottle

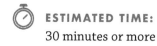

SUPPLIES NEEDED:
Paper and Pen
Bottle

ESTIMATED TIME:
30 minutes or more

You already know who you're kissing today, so this isn't your typical game of Spin the Bottle. It is, however, a nice way to spice up your evening or even get some tasks done around the house in the most delightful manner.

INSTRUCTIONS

1. Draw a circle with six or more sections on a sheet of paper using this example as a guide. Write down an action in each section, using the example for inspiration. The actions can be sweet, sexy, silly, or practical, like chores that need to be done around the house.

2. Decide which partner spins first. Lay the bottle in the middle of the circle and spin the bottle. Whatever the bottle points to must be done by the player. Then it's the other person's turn. If the action is a chore that'll take a while to finish, you can keep a record of things to complete when the game is over. Keep playing as long as you'd like.

Do the
Dishes

Kiss
on the
Cheek

Give a Sweet
Compliment

Tidy up
(Partner chooses
the Room)

Kiss
for 30
Seconds

1-Minute
Back Rub

Be Weird

Do you celebrate each other's weirdness? Can you be unabashedly silly together in public? Let's find out. Warning: If you hate calling attention to yourselves, this activity may be outside of your and your partner's comfort zones. Give it a try and feel free to adjust to suit your own personalities.

INSTRUCTIONS

1. Go out and be weird together!

   Suggestions:

   • Go to a public place and dance around with unplugged headphones. Swing the cord around so it's obvious they're not connected to anything.

   • Set a table with a tablecloth and silverware in a casual café. Dress up like you're going to prom or your own wedding.

   • Sing an acapella duet and see if anyone joins you.

   • Ask a stranger what year it is, then turn to your partner with a look of shock when they tell you.

2. Watch for the reactions you receive. You and your partner will be able to laugh about it together later, especially if you take notes below.

What We Did: _____

How People Reacted: _____

_____

_____

_____

Creative

Creating together is a wonderful way to wind down and relax while also staying engaged with one another, making it a better option than binge watching a show (at least some of the time!). If zany songs, cheesy art projects, and making (and eating!) cookies sound like some of the best ways to spend your afternoon or evening, you'll love this chapter. You'll have the opportunity to make things together, dress each other up (going out that way is optional), and enjoy each other's company. You could even combine two or more activities for the ultimate creative date.

Love Song Parody

 SUPPLIES NEEDED:
Smartphone
Computer with internet connection
Pen
Paper

ESTIMATED TIME: 30 minutes to 1+ hours
(more if you make a video)

This is a fun, silly way to relive the butterflies you felt when you first met and started dating. Plus, you'll have a unique "Our Song." It may never play on the radio while you're driving or dancing the way other couples' songs do (unless you record yourselves!), but you can sing and laugh your way through your own version together whenever you hear the original.

INSTRUCTIONS

1. Reminisce about the first time you met and how you became a couple.

2. Choose a fun song you both enjoy or find catchy and pull up the lyrics to use as a guide. Start with the first verse or go straight to the chorus (sometimes that's an easier starting point), and write your love story as a song parody. Play up the humorous moments and make it as hilariously absurd as possible while sticking to your general story.

Things to consider:

Where did you meet? _____

What were you wearing? _____

First impressions? _____

Who was around? _____

What were you doing? _____

What happened on the first date? _____

How did you feel after the first date was over? _____

_____

TIP: If you're feeling especially creative and maybe even silly, pull up the karaoke version of the song on YouTube and make your own music video once you have written the lyrics.

Write your parody lyrics here:

_____

_____

_____

_____

_____

_____

_____

_____

_____

_____

_____

_____

_____

_____

_____

_____

Creating by Hand, Together

 SUPPLIES NEEDED:
Varies, depending on project

ESTIMATED TIME: 1 to 2 hours, depending on project

How well do you work together when you're creating something new? Each partner has their own strengths and weaknesses, which can make it easy to divide and conquer daily tasks independently. However, spending time to create something with someone you care about can teach you to combine those characteristics in a beautiful new way.

INSTRUCTIONS

1. Choose something you'd both like to make, create, or design that isn't exactly in either of your wheelhouses. It should be something you're both interested in and have roughly the same amount of experience with. Ideally you would both have limited experience, but enough to have some supplies lying around that you can use.

    Ideas include:

    *   Baking a cake

    *   Pottery (ahem, think of a certain sexy clay-handling scene)

    *   Scrapbooking

    *   Oil painting

    *   Cooking a new type of cuisine

    *   Building a bookshelf

    If one of you is already an expert, you may end up with teacher/student or leader/follower dynamic, so it's important to choose something you're equally unfamiliar with.

2. Come up with your plan and gather your supplies, including any necessary instructions.

3. Work *closely* together to complete the project, making sure you're both putting in equal effort.

4. Log your project ideas here and check them off as you complete them together.

☐ _____

☐ _____

☐ _____

☐ _____

☐ _____

☐ _____

☐ _____

☐ _____

☐ _____

☐ _____

☐ _____

☐ _____

☐ _____

☐ _____

☐ _____

☐ _____

☐ _____

☐ _____

☐ _____

Our Cookie Recipe

 SUPPLIES NEEDED:

A basic cookie recipe and the ingredients

Cookie add-ins

Mixing bowl

Spatula

Baking sheet

Oven

Icing and sprinkles, for decorating (optional)

ESTIMATED TIME: 45 minutes

Now that you have a special song together (see page 104), why not add a signature cookie recipe to define your relationship? Celebrate your originality, work together to create something great, and then enjoy your sweet snack.

INSTRUCTIONS

1. Find a basic cookie recipe you think you'd both enjoy. Try looking for recipes for sugar cookies, oatmeal cookies, or chocolate chip cookies. Make the dough as directed.

2. Decide what really makes these cookies "you" as a couple. If you love chocolate and your significant other loves pistachios, fold chocolate chips and pistachios into the dough. Is there anything else you could add that might complement the flavors you've already chosen? Peanut butter? Butterscotch? Dried cranberries? Walnuts?

3. Chill the dough if necessary, then roll it into balls and bake as directed.

4. Let the cookies cool, then either enjoy eating them right away or take some time to decorate them in a way that represents your relationship.

5. Write your recipe here for posterity.

RECIPE

RECIPE NAME_____

SERVINGS_____   PREP TIME_____

INGREDIENTS

_____   _____

_____   _____

_____   _____

_____   _____

_____   _____

_____   _____

DIRECTIONS

_____

_____

_____

_____

_____

_____

_____

Have a Silly Photo Shoot

 SUPPLIES NEEDED:
Silly props (optional)
Camera or phone camera
Tripod or selfie stick (optional)

ESTIMATED TIME: 10+ minutes

Show off your personalities in a no-rules photo shoot that you can keep to yourselves or share with the world later. This is where you can really let your creativity and silliness soar.

INSTRUCTIONS

1. Decide on a photo shoot location, create or gather any props you will use, and pick out your outfits. Coordinate your clothes if that's your style, or just do this spontaneously and wear what you have on right now.

2. Set up a tripod for your camera or mount your phone on a selfie stick, if you're using one, or get close to each other to make some silly faces for selfies.

3. Take turns taking pics of each other without the tripod or selfie stick to get action shots.

4. If you want to share them, post them on social media, or save them for your next round of holiday cards or a big announcement.

5. Print and save your favorites here, or place them on your refrigerator or in a frame.

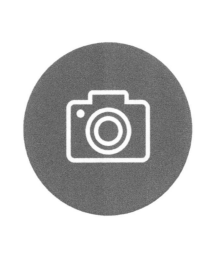

Handprint Craft Keepsake

Newspaper

Canvas

Kid-safe tempera or acrylic paint in two colors

Paper plates

Pencil

Permanent marker or paint pen

🕐 **ESTIMATED TIME:** 30 minutes

Why should handprint keepsakes be reserved for babies and toddlers? Create your own handprint keepsake as a lasting reminder of your love for each other.

INSTRUCTIONS

1. Cover a table with newspaper to protect the surface and place the canvas on top.

2. Pour the paint onto two paper plates—one for each color—enough to cover each person's hand.

3. The person with larger hands should go first. Dip one hand into the paint, with fingers fully stretched to ensure the hand is completely covered with a thin layer of paint from the base of the palm to each fingertip.

4. Press the hand into the canvas gently, applying consistent pressure, and then lift the hand off the canvas. Be careful not to smudge the paint.

5. The other partner repeats steps 4 and 5 using a second color of paint but pressing the hand slightly overlapping the fingers of the first partner's print.

6. Below the handprints sketch in pencil first, "Holding hands since [year you started dating]." Once you're satisfied with the lettering, go over it with a permanent marker or paint pen. Let it dry and then put it on display.

HEY
HOT
STUFF

You're
so Hot

SPICE
THINGS UP

YOU SET MY
EVERYTHING
ON FIRE

HOT CHILLI SAUCE!

HOT

YOU SPICE
UP MY LIFE

tomato

CHAPTER THIRTEEN

Spicy

Every couple that's been together for a while occasionally looks to heat things up in their relationship. Spice things up (sometimes literally!) with the activities in this chapter. Sample a new dish that really takes advantage of the wide variety of spices in the world (and maybe even doubles as an aphrodisiac), or try on a sexy new "come hither" stare that'll make your partner melt.

Make a Spicy Meal Together

SUPPLIES NEEDED:
Recipe for a spicy meal
Ingredients for your recipe(s) of choice
Tools to prepare and cook the food

ESTIMATED TIME: 45+ minutes, depending on the recipe

Some say spicy food is an aphrodisiac. Heat things up with a dish that contains chiles, cayenne, cinnamon, chili powder, or other warming spices.

INSTRUCTIONS

1. Choose your spicy cuisine. Mexican, Thai, and Indian recipes are a good (and tasty) place to start. You could pick a recipe for a full meal, like a curry dish or tacos with an extra spicy kick, or go with a spicy chocolate dessert.

2. Shop for ingredients for your recipe as necessary.

3. Prepare and cook the meal together.

4. Set the table and feed each other a couple of bites before you dig into your spicy meal.

Here's a quick, spicy snack to get you started:

Ingredients:

1 teaspoon cinnamon
Pinch salt
Pinch ground cayenne
Chili powder, to taste

1 tablespoon cocoa powder
2 tablespoons melted coconut oil
3 tablespoons honey
½ cup raw whole almonds

1. In a medium bowl, combine the cinnamon, salt, cayenne, chili powder, and cocoa powder.

2. Add the coconut oil and honey and stir to combine.

3. Add the almonds and stir until they are covered.

4. Spread the coated almonds evenly on a baking sheet and drizzle any remaining liquid over them.

5. Chill the almonds in the refrigerator or freezer. They taste better and are less messy when cold.

6. Once cool, feed them to each other.

TIP: If spicy foods aren't your thing, there are other aphrodisiac foods to try! Get creative with chocolate, raspberries, avocados, almonds, or even asparagus.

Come Hither Looks

⏱ ESTIMATED TIME: 2 minutes

Give your partner your sexiest "come hither" look. The flirtier, the better. *Warning*: This one could go from "spicy" to "silly" if you keep it going. Have fun and see what happens.

INSTRUCTIONS

1. Practice giving each other your best "come hither" looks. Don't just stop at one look each! See who can pull off a seductive vibe most successfully without laughing.

   Hint: The more intense the look is, the more likely it is to inspire at least a giggle.

2. Make sure you remember which steamy expressions have the biggest impact and are deemed the sexiest so you and your significant other will be ready to spring those looks on each other later when they're unsuspecting.

3. When you're ready to heat things up, see how well it works.

Roll the Dice

 SUPPLIES NEEDED:
Dice
Pen or pencil

🕑 **ESTIMATED TIME:** 15 to 20 minutes

This activity is designed to prompt some outside-the-box actions between the two of you. It's customizable based on what you choose to write in. Roll the dice . . . and see where the evening takes you.

INSTRUCTIONS

1. Fill in the numbered Action and Body Part lists below. Some of the actions could include massage, kiss, draw, tickle, give a funny name, and write a short poem. Feel free to get creative.

2. Decide who will roll first. The first partner rolls the die to choose a corresponding action, then rolls it again to determine the body part that action will be applied to.

3. The other partner then has to perform the action (so they may have to write a verse of poetry about their lover's elbow, for example). Then it's their turn to roll the die. Keep going as long as you'd like.

4. Feel free to mark through or erase your first set of responses below, change them, and continue to play.

Action   Body Part

⚀ _____   ⚀ _____

⚁ _____   ⚁ _____

⚂ _____   ⚂ _____

⚃ _____   ⚃ _____

⚄ _____   ⚄ _____

⚅ _____   ⚅ _____

Dress Up for Two

⊂═▷ SUPPLIES NEEDED:
Clothes from your closets
Accessories (optional)
Makeup (optional)

🕐 **ESTIMATED TIME:** 20 minutes, not including meal, activity, or driving (if you choose to go out)

Do you trust your partner to choose your clothing, accessories, and maybe even makeup? What will their choices reveal? What exciting new looks (or hilarity) will ensue?

INSTRUCTIONS

1. Decide where you're going, if anywhere, so you both have guidelines for this activity. The goal isn't to embarrass your partner, unless you both decide it is! If you're staying in for date night, the risks for embarrassment are lower but the possibilities for attire are endless, and you may end up wearing something pretty wacky for a few hours.

2. Go into each other's closets and choose outfits and accessories for each other. If you wear makeup and have a collection to choose from, have your partner select your makeup colors and products.

3. Get dressed, using everything your partner selected for you, and go on your date.

4. Take a picture of your outfits together and save it here as a keepsake.

TIP: If you want to branch out from what's in your closets, you can always hit up a thrift store or other store that sells inexpensive items to add a little pizzazz to what you'll be wearing.

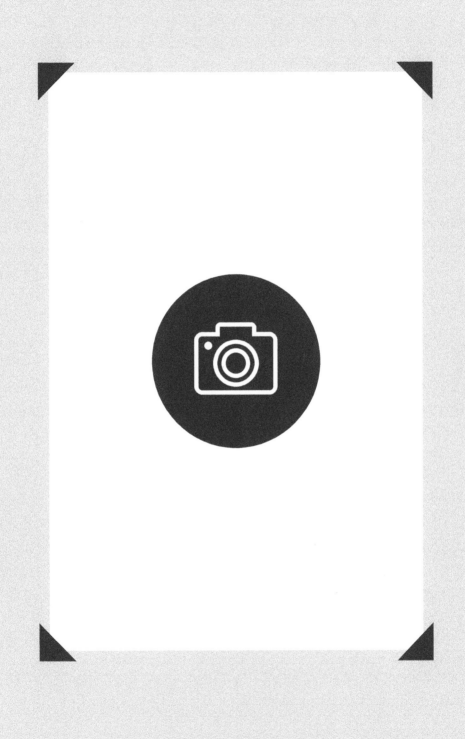

Learn to Tango Online

SUPPLIES NEEDED:
Dress, suit, and appropriate shoes (don't start with very high heels, though)
Access to dance lessons online

ESTIMATED TIME: 45 minutes to 1 hour or more over several sessions

Throw your passion into movement as you learn to tango, one of the most sensual forms of dance. You can learn from online instructors for free and go at your own pace. Check out the resources (see page 134) for online course suggestions. You'll need more than one night to learn the dance, of course, so put these sensual date nights on the calendar at least once per week for a couple of months.

INSTRUCTIONS

1. Get dressed in your sexy dance attire, if preferred, and preview some free dance lessons online.

2. Decide which instructors you and your partner find the easiest to follow. You can watch them on a computer screen and follow along if necessary. However, if you're able to stream the videos on your television, you'll probably find it even easier to follow the steps.

3. Practice for as long as you'd like for your first session, then decide how often you want to incorporate practice into your lives. Maybe you want a quick, daily practice. Maybe you can only work it in during your weekly date nights. There's no wrong way to plan it. Enjoy the routine of learning something new together.

TIP: If you already know how to tango or would like an alternative, try learning salsa, bachata, or rumba.

CHAPTER FOURTEEN

Outdoorsy and Active

Sunlight, physical activity, and quality time are all mood boosters, so spending time together outside in the sun is a fantastic way to strengthen your bond and help your love grow. Use this chapter for inspiration and go soak up some vitamin D or get a little exercise with your significant other. Run, dance, tour the town on foot, plant a garden together, or go on a picnic somewhere quiet and private. In some cases, you'll even be able to do good in the world by raising money for a charity, supporting small businesses, or planting your own food.

Run or Walk a 5K Together

SUPPLIES NEEDED:

Internet connection (optional)

Smartphones (optional)

Running or walking shoes

Comfortable clothes

Access to treadmills (optional)

Water bottles

ESTIMATED TIME: 30 minutes to 1½ hours

Support a good cause together by getting out and getting active. You can do this by running a race in your community or by recording it virtually (this one makes it doable if you're in a long-distance relationship or there are no current local races).

INSTRUCTIONS

1. Sign up for a race or run in or near your town.

2. If there isn't a race coming up locally, find a virtual run online at GoneForaRun.com, VirtualRunEvents.com, or just do a quick search in your web browser to find one you'd both like to run.

3. Don running shoes and comfortable clothes. Map your 5K route using a site like Runkeeper.com, or run it on treadmills at the gym. If you're already runners, you can sign up for longer races.

4. Use this as an opportunity to train together regularly before the real event and download the Charity Miles app to raise money as you rack up the practice run miles. Don't forget your water bottles!

Have a Dance Party at Home

 SUPPLIES NEEDED:
Music and something to play it on
Smartphone (optional)

ESTIMATED TIME: As much time as you want to spend on it

There are no rules, no designated steps to learn, no teachers to follow, and no specific playlists for this one. The only limits are your musical tastes and how much room you have to move your bodies. If your dance moves are terrible, even better. You'll be laughing together in no time.

INSTRUCTIONS

1. Turn your music on and turn it up!

2. If you want to create your own special playlist for the occasion, take a few minutes to do so. You can brainstorm and write a list on this page, then add them to Spotify, Pandora, or another music-playing option later.

3. Dance together and show each other your dance moves, whether they're good or bad. Be ridiculous. Teach each other new moves you just made up. See how many you can string together (taking turns, one unusual dance move at a time) and memorize to create your own crazy dance.

Dance Party Playlist:

_____

_____

_____

_____

_____

_____

Plant a Garden for Two

 SUPPLIES NEEDED:

Pen

Seeds or young plants

Containers and/or space
for planting in your yard
(with the right amount of
sunlight for what you're
planting)

Soil

Watering cans or a hose

Shovel

Fertilizer

ESTIMATED TIME: 30 minutes to several hours, depending on what—and how much—you choose to plant

Let your love grow! Create your own garden together—whether it's large and full of vegetables, a small indoor assortment of microgreens and/or herbs, or simply bunches of flowers to make things prettier.

INSTRUCTIONS

1. Sit down together and decide what you'd like to grow in the space you have available. Research which types of plants can flourish in your home. List your ideas below.

2. Buy the seeds or young plants and gather equipment, such as containers, soil, water cans, a shovel, and fertilizer. Set aside a section of time one afternoon to plant the seeds.

3. If you live together, decide how you'll split the tasks involved in caring for your plants. When the time comes (and assuming you didn't only plant flowers), you can center another date around using food you've grown together in a recipe.

TIP: If you're limited on space and don't have a yard of your own, you can plant a container garden or grow microgreens or herbs like mint, cilantro, or basil indoors in small pots by a window.

To Plant:

_____   _____

_____   _____

_____   _____

_____   _____

_____   _____

_____   _____

_____   _____

_____   _____

_____   _____

Be Tourists in Your Own Town

 SUPPLIES NEEDED:

Pen

Mode of transportation

Tickets to things you want to see or do (optional)

Camera (optional)

ESTIMATED TIME: 1 hour or more

See your town with fresh eyes! Do some or all of the things you've been meaning to do since you first moved there—the things tourists might do that residents tend to forget or neglect in favor of the demands and routines of daily life. Don't forget to take pictures like you're on vacation!

INSTRUCTIONS

1. Make a list of things to do and see below. Is there a museum, park, or restaurant you've always said you'd visit "later"? Now's the time.

2. Map out a plan to fit as many of your itinerary items into the day or weekend as you can. You may discover that you've missed out on many things that you need to break it up into multiple dates, due to time or cost. Number them so you can plan your route(s). Dress comfortably and get started. Don't forget to take pictures!

Things to Do and See:

_____ _____

_____ _____

_____ _____

_____ _____

_____ _____

_____ _____

Have a Picnic

 SUPPLIES NEEDED:
Food
Beverages
Basket or cooler

ESTIMATED TIME: 1 hour or more

Enjoy some gorgeous scenery and your loved one's company any time of the day. Whether impromptu or planned, a picnic never fails to be a relaxing and lovely activity to do together. Below you'll find some ideas and prompts to help one come together.

INSTRUCTIONS

1. Pack a picnic basket or cooler with food and drinks before you head out to a beautiful spot by the water, in a park, or even in your backyard. There's no rule that says this has to be a lunchtime picnic, either.

2. If you two like to get up early or you've been longing to watch the sunrise together, program your coffee maker before dawn, heat up some breakfast burritos or the overnight oats you prepped the day before, and head outside with your breakfast and coffee while it's still dark. Enjoy the quiet, peaceful first hours of the day together.

3. Another option—and an easier one for night owls—is to watch the sun go down during an evening picnic. Pack some fruit, a variety of cheeses, sandwiches, other snacks, and drinks and head out to the park after work.

Answer Key

Across:

1. Romance
2. Red
3. App
4. Flirt
5. Yes
6. Once
7. Aims

Down:

1. Conversation
2. Candy
3. Feelings
4. Smile
5. Cuddle

CHAPTER FOUR: SCRAMBLED
WORDS OF AFFECTION

You are the best
I'm so lucky
Hug me
Kiss me
You are so cute
Wanna date
Movie night
Can't wait to see you again
You make me so happy
Forever isn't long enough
Favorite person
Love you lots

Happiness
Soulmates
Hold my hand

CHAPTER TEN: SEEING
THE FUTURE

Resources

Books

***A Year of Us: A Couples Journal: One Question a Day to Spark Fun and Meaningful Conversations* by Alicia Muñoz, LPC**
This book offers a quick way to reconnect each day for a year and may prompt discussions you wouldn't have had on your own.

***Relationship Workbook for Couples: A Guide to Deeper Connection, Trust, and Intimacy for Couples—Young and Old* by Rachel Stone**
If you've got the fun side of connection covered and want something deeper and more serious, this book offers tips on communication and getting to know each other better on several levels.

***The Couple's Quiz Book: 350 Fun Questions to Energize Your Relationship* by Alicia Muñoz, LPC**
Working through this book (a companion to this one!) will encourage you to get to know each other very well. Instead of only presenting questions, it explains why it's important to know the answers.

***The Five Love Languages: The Secret to Love that Lasts* by Gary Chapman**
You and your partner may share a mutual and deep love, yet sometimes it doesn't always feel that way because everyone shows and feels love in different ways. This book helps you understand and navigate those differences.

Websites

LoveToKnow Dating & Relationships (Dating.LovetoKnow.com)
There's something for every kind of relationship here, from advice to more ways to have fun together.

Psychology Today's Relationships section (PsychologyToday.com /us/basics/relationships)
You can browse the interesting articles and get insights into the inner workings of relationships.

The Dating Divas (TheDatingDivas.com)
You can find a plethora of date ideas, gifts, and challenges here.

Your Tango's Love section (YourTango.com/love)
Get advice and inspiration that could take your relationship to the next level.

Activity Resources

CHAPTER TWO

DIY Escape Room
- If you love the idea of an escape room but need some inspiration, this post can kickstart your imagination: BigEscapeRooms .com/design-an-escape-room-game.

International Love Languages
- Google Translate: Use this free app on your smartphone or access the website on any device. It will even say the word or phrase out loud for you if you don't know how to pronounce it.
- iTranslate: You can use the basic version of this app for free; this should be enough for activities in this book.

CHAPTER FIVE

Compliments from Around the World
- Google Translate: Use this free app on your smartphone or access the website on any device. It will even say the word or phrase out loud for you if you don't know how to pronounce it.

- iTranslate: You can use the basic version of this app for free; this should be enough for activities in this book.

Get Your Dancing Shoes On
- Howcast.com: You can find videos that will help you learn the tango, fox-trot, cha-cha, rumba, samba, and more. These short videos can walk you through the basic dance steps.
- LearnToDance.com: You can learn the basic steps to several different dances here, sometimes in the form of multivideo mini-courses. If you and your partner find a dance you really enjoy, you'll have the option to purchase lessons that go into more detail.
- YouTube is another free resource to try when you're new to a dance. Channels like DanceClassVideo, Passion4dancing, Addicted2Salsa, and Ballroom Mastery TV can be a tremendous help when you're just starting to learn a new dance.

CHAPTER SIX

Make a Time Capsule
You'll find tips on how to make the most of your time capsule. It includes information about which materials could increase the chances of its survival: FuturePkg.com/7-time-capsule -preservation-secrets-revealed.
- You can get additional preservation tips here: MNHS.org /preserve/conservation/reports/timecapsule.pdf.

CHAPTER EIGHT

Around the World, Tapas-Style
Here's a variety of cookbook recommendations if you need some inspiration:
- *Cook Like a Local* by Chris Shepherd and Kaitlyn Goalen
- *Cooking Light Global Kitchen* by David Joachim and The Editors of Cooking Light

- *Gluten Free World Tour Cookbook* by Katie Moseman
- *Together: Our Community Cookbook* by The Hubb Community Kitchen
- *We Are La Cocina* by Caleb Zigas and Leticia Landa

CHAPTER NINE

Couple's Meditation Time

- Insight Timer app: There are 40,000 free and searchable meditation and music tracks to choose from.
- Oak-Meditation & Breathing app: This free app has guided and unguided meditations, breathing exercises, and nature sounds that will help you fall asleep.
- YouTube is another good resource for free guided meditations and nature sounds. Check out the channel YouTube.com/calm for short guided meditations, sleep meditations, and nature sounds you can use for an unguided meditation.

CHAPTER THIRTEEN

Learn to Tango Online

- Howcast.com: You can find videos that will help you learn the tango, fox-trot, cha-cha, rumba, samba, and more. These short videos can walk you through the basic dance steps.
- LearnToDance.com: You can learn the basic steps to several different dances here, sometimes in the form of multivideo mini-courses. If you and your partner find a dance you really enjoy, you'll have the option to purchase lessons that go into more detail.
- YouTube is another free resource to try when you're new to a dance. Channels like DanceClassVideo, Passion4dancing, Addicted2Salsa, and Ballroom Mastery TV can be a tremendous help when you're just starting to learn a new dance.

About the Author

 **Crystal Schwanke** has been a freelance writer, blogger, ghostwriter, and copywriter since 2005. In 2004, she graduated from Valdosta State University with a bachelor of arts in psychology. She's done everything from sales copy and product descriptions to magazine articles and web content for a variety of publications, including LoveToKnow .com, WritersWeekly.com, *Fayette Woman* magazine, and Babble.com. She's the creator of *That Old Kitchen Table*, a blog designed to help women live joyful, fulfilling lives. She lives in the Atlanta, Georgia, area with her husband, daughter, and a rescued pit bull named Josephine. When she's not writing or spending time with family, she's reading, working out, and going down coffee-fueled research rabbit holes. Find Crystal online at:

ThatOldKitchenTable.com

Facebook.com/thatoldkitchentable

Instagram.com/thatoldkitchentable

CPSIA information can be obtained
at www.ICGtesting.com
Printed in the USA
JSHW020425230122
22170JS00002B/2